LADY OF THE STARS

STEVIE NICKS

LADY OF

THE

STARS

STEVIE NICKS

by Edward Wincentsen

Wynn Publishing

WYNN PUBLISHING
P.O. Box 1491
Pickens, SC (29671)
U.S.A.

First Edition

©1995 Wynn Publishing & Edward Wincentsen
Library of Congress Catalog Card Number: 94-090560
ISBN: 0-9642808-0-9

Book Cover Concept: Ed Wincentsen
Book Cover Design: Gary Ward
Book Design: Ed Wincentsen

PRINTED IN THE U.S.A.

**Dedicated
to
Jean Enloe**

Introduction

"As long as I can play a song and people are still sitting there at the end of it, I won't worry about my music losing value."

Thus, Stevie Nicks answered the critics, in *People Magazine,* June 13, 1994, concerning the question if she was out of date with the current music trends upon the release of her new album, *Street Angel.*

Some of the critics can be biting indeed. As the Daily News writer Glen Kenny wrote July 17, 1994, "If there is any analogue to *Sunset Boulevard's* Norma Desmond in rock, it must be Stevie Nicks. Imagine Stevie roaming through her mansion swaddled in frilly fabric, believing that the world outside is still held in thrall by the Maxfield Parrish-tinted visions of the glazed-eyed doe this middle-aged woman no longer is. Her latest solo album, *Street Angel,* is the aural equivalent to that clueless anachronistic script Desmond sends to Cecil B. DeMille in one of Sunset's wrenching embarrassments."

Is Stevie Nicks caught up in her own delusions and crystal visions? She has stated that she is not concerned if her music does not reflect the popular fads going today. And, I would agree that music is music, no matter what time period it is. Consider Elvis Presley. His music will continue to be heard down through the years. Of course, Stevie's answer may not reflect the current market place in today's world of hip/hop, rap, heavy metal or alternative. Time will tell how well *Street Angel* will sell, and perhaps reflect how strong her following still is. Music critics should not be fooled, Stevie Nicks still has a very large, loyal following. I will get into my own personal observations of *Street Angel* later in this book.

For reader's who are aware of my first book on Stevie entitled, *Stevie Nicks, Rock's Mystical Lady,* the question may arise on why a second book? One answer is that she is a fascinating subject and much could be devoted to her as a subject. Another answer is that I wanted to bring the story up to date with the release of her long awaited new album and that I had more things to say that I didn't get to on the first book. There are more answers also that I will just keep quiet about, keep a mystique about it as Stevie is so good at doing.

I did want to approach this book in a little different kind of a slant, a more personal journalistic style. To be able to share some of my own personal experiences about my pitfalls and problems that I encountered as I researched and worked on the first book.

All reading material must be evaluated with a discerning mind because the writer may be tinting the material, not only with their own views and slant, but sometimes even with more sinister motives in mind. This book, as my first one on Stevie Nicks was, is *not* a gossip, or tell-all book. It could have been, but that is not my purpose here. I want to present Stevie Nicks as the artist, this time being more objective and presenting some of both the positive and negative that I have observed. The reader needs to read it with that "discerning mind."

I continue to be a fan of Stevie Nicks and her music. In my eyes she is a poet, a dreamer and a gifted songwriter who can cast spells with her music. Her music has touched many people and given them hope, and in some instances *miracles*.

I have letters from readers of my first book who have shared such stories. Is her music relevant for today, will it hold up and endure into the future when we are gone from this planet? Will Stevie's music be as some of the great poet's works, enduring down through time, her music being a document of popular culture and a voice from this time? Perhaps the dreamers and poets of today can answer that, I cannot. As she says in her song *Destiny* from *Street Angel*, " ... my destiny is fighting again, secretly unwinding, what it was that I was supposed to say, to say to you today."

Edward Wincentsen
August 1994
Tulsa, Oklahoma

Photo: Joe Sia

Stevie Nicks, Gypsy Poet

"**I**'ll never run myself into the ground again, because I don't think it's fair to my spirit or my body or the people that love my music or my family or anybody else to kill myself over this. Someday, I think I'd rather sit in a rocking chair and write the songs and maybe even go to the Roxy (club in Los Angeles) and sing them and put them on a record."

And how far off is that time?

"I'd say probably about four years."

That quote by Stevie Nicks was made to the *Arizona Republic* newspaper writer, Andrew Means, in December 5, 1981. Well, Stevie Nicks is still doing her music today. As of this writing she just released her latest solo album, *Street Angel.*

However, it seems that Stevie has always had a realistic look at how long she can keep performing in public. It does seem that she will always be writing songs though, from her comments of past and present. The magazine *High Times* asked her in March of 1982 about it. "HT: You've said that in middle age, you'd like to be on top of a mountain with a piano and a typewriter. Nicks: I would, I look forward to that. I love my performing and I'll do that for another five or six years, but there will be a point in my life when what I'll really want to do is go away and write. And I'll write about all of this. I've already written thousands of pages. The story's written already. I'll want to add to it and I want to put it together and it'll be an incredible book."

In *Bam Magazine,* September 11, 1981, she stated similar things concerning songwriting and performing in connection to her *Bella Donna* album, "I'm far too intelligent to not know that there will be a time when I won't be 33 anymore, when I won't be that pretty anymore, I won't be sparkly anymore, and I'll be tired. I want to be able to know that I can still have fun and be part of the world, and that I didn't give it all away for Fleetwood Mac. That's what *Bella Donna* is all about. It's the beginning of my life."

✠

My story began around 1991 when I was considering doing a book on Stevie Nicks. Eventually, after many setbacks and much work we were able to complete the first book, *Stevie Nicks, Rock's Mystical Lady* in 1993. One of the key people who was involved with the book project was a woman by the name of Jean Enloe. I got acquainted with Jean through a fan publication she was doing entitled, *Platform* (based on the type of shoes Stevie wears). Jean had connections to Stevie and I had had no success up to that point in time dealing with Stevie's management about the book. Jean and I continued to correspond and talk on the telephone about my idea for the book. I eventually went out to Los Angeles to work with Jean for two weeks in January of 1993.

Jean was an incredible archivist of Stevie materials and a avid collector. She was sought out by people doing any kind of projects on Fleetwood Mac, or Stevie, for her knowledge and expertise. I learned of Jean's involvement with some of Stevie's family, especially of her friendship with Stevie's mother Barbara. Jean and Barbara would talk on the telephone three to four times a week, or more, they also shared a common concern, having heart conditions. Of course Jean was a devout follower of Stevie and had had numerous meetings with Stevie. One thing that was interesting was that Stevie asked Jean if she would cease publication of *Platform*. In a letter from Jenny (the person who answers Stevie's fan mail) she states how there are numerous **unauthorized** fan magazines out and that **only** Stevie and her brother are **authorized** to do such publications.

Jean did stop the publication of *Platform* due to her devotion to Stevie and wanting to always stay on the good side of her, but I knew that Jean was sad about having to do this. Then Jean would also do errands for Stevie, such as get esoteric books for Stevie from the New Age bookstore called the *Bodhi Tree Bookstore.* Stevie would always want to give certain books out to friends and would buy numbers of copies of a certain title. I learned through my time with Jean that Stevie helped put a certain relative, (by marriage) through a drug and alcohol rehab program, paying for all the costs herself. Jean would also baby-sit the children of one of Stevie's cousins who had embraced Buddhist teaching. I met him on two occasions at Jean's Los Angeles apartment.

One of my chief aims was to try to get Stevie's involvement with the book, but I finally received the definite "No" on one of the last days I was working with Jean. I had gone to Los Angeles with a business partner and we had asked Jean if she would ask Stevie's mother if the two of us could stop at their home in Scottsdale, Arizona (Stevie's parents home) to talk about the book. This was after many unsuccessful attempts to have Stevie's former management help out on the book. Jean received a phone call from Barbara Nicks telling her that the answer was "No" for our visit. The word had come from Stevie's personal assistant, via her management.

One of the objections to my request for help on the book, either from Stevie's management, or from Stevie was that, "Why should Stevie help you on a book when she is working on her own book?" According to the Press Release materials from *Modern* and *Atlantic Records* in connection to Stevie's *Street Angel* album it says that "... she (Stevie) is in the process of putting together a book entitled *Dreams, Stories, and Poems,* culled largely from the journals she's kept over the years; aside from her writings, it will also include some of her drawings and photographs."

MARJORIE NICHOLAS
"Music Man" 1,
STEPHANIE NICKS
Players Club 4; "High Spirits" 4.
HENRY NOBLE

Stevie's High School
Class of 1966

14

I've heard and read in interviews about this book that is suppose to come out for more than five or six years now.

If the book does come out it will surely be a big treat for all her fans, including myself.

In *Hit Parader Magazine,* September 1983, writers Stan Hyman and Vicki Greenleaf in their article, *Stevie Nicks Magic Touch* stated, "Also in the works for Nicks is a book. A diary of sorts, it will include handpainted photographs. A friend of Nicks' is reproducing the print in calligraphy on parchment paper. "I just write a page every night," Nicks said. "You wouldn't believe the thousands of pages of stuff that I have. I just jot down what's happening. I'll get to say everything I ever wanted to say," she said laughing. "So, I'm real excited. The book people told me, "You don't have to sing anymore if you don't want to. You can just stop and write books." I've never seen that book come about.

Then in the *Music Connection Magazine,* the January 9-22, 1989 issue, writer, Laura Gross in an article entitled, *Fleetwood Mac's Leading Ladies: Stevie Nicks & Christine McVie,* asked, "MC: Does that mean we'll never see your poetry published? SN: I'm trying. I'm working on it, I really am. It's been so busy for the last year. I still write, but I don't want to go back and edit it. I just want to keep writing.... . I have about 150 drawings that I've done in the last five years. But I don't like to finish them, just like I don't like to finish books. And I really don't even like to finish songs, because then they're done, and they're handed over to somebody else. As long as they're still not quite finished, whether it's a song or a painting, or anything — it's still mine."

So I guess that fans will have to wait to see if this book that *Modern* and *Atlantic* is talking about, *Dreams, Stories, and Poems* will indeed materialize.

In my first book I related how Stevie's songwriting inspiration sometimes comes from reading her favorite writers and poets. I had quoted from Jenny Boyd's book, *Musicians In Tune,* "Sometimes I'll get out of bed in the middle of night and go into my office and put the paper in the typewriter and get out my books that are inspirational to me — Oscar Wilde, Keats, Canadian poets, European poets — and I'll just open a page and read something, and I'll say, "Okay, this is my information for today, this is what is supposed to come through me today," and I'll close the book, so I'll never be able to find that page again, and I'll think about it for awhile, and then I'll probably write for one or two hours, then I'll be able to go back to bed."

Again, in Andrew Means *Arizona Republic* newspaper article of December 5, 1981 it reads, "She describes her writing style as "journalistic."

"I write at night in prose," she said. "I write what's happening in my life down in somewhat of a formal prose way and then I go back and I put anything that I think is important into rhyme."

Many times it appears in her songs that the characters may well be herself. As she referred to this part of her songwriting in an article entitled *Through the Glass Darkly* written by Sylvie Simmons for Revolution magazine, November 1989, Stevie bears this out concerning her *Other Side of the Mirror* album, "I love making up little fantasy things," Stevie says. "All the characters in my songs — the Gypsies, the Saras, and on this album, Alice and Juliet — they'll all me. But they're all different sides of me. It's a great way to write about what's going on in your life without telling it in a real serious way, but the point comes over and I think people understand that."

Also in the same article concerning songwriting Stevie gave this interesting observation about herself, "They may think of me as a certain image. "Well, she's kind of airy-fairy and she probably flies around her house in black chiffon," Stevie bristles, "which is all not really very true. But, on the

17

other side of it, the fact is that part of me **is** that way. There is a part of me that has to depend on fantasy, because if you can't be somewhat of a fantasy person, then you can't write. If you can't believe in dreams, then you can't believe that things will work out, so what are you going to write about?"

As I had mentioned in my first book I had hours and hours of unrelated songs, demos and music of Stevie to listen to and saw what a talent she has for songwriting from these raw recordings. I had gotten these from Jean Enloe, and have since erased them. In a bio/ promotional piece from *Atlantic and Modern Records* in regards to her *Other Side of the Mirror* album Stevie is quoted as saying, "A lot of my friends tend to go back and listen to the demos of my songs before they went on to be records and they're told me they like the feel of those." I saw this in her recordings, a quality that is sometimes missed with lots of heavy production. I think her new album *Street Angel* comes the closest to this more pure form of production without so much studio tampering than any in many years, capturing some of this innocent essence.

In another interview by *Modern and Atlantic Records* by Dan Neer and James Fahey Stevie gave some revealing thoughts on songwriting, "For anybody who really wants to say something, music is a great way to do it because it will get past a lot of bridges you'll never get past if you're speaking. If you're singing, they'll let you go past the toll bridge without probably even charging you."

On the *USA Today* cable television program Stevie said to Mary Wallace on June 3rd, 1989, "I'll always still sneak through a little bit of music and a little bit of philosophy and a little bit of teaching somehow (in her music)."

In the next section I will show how Stevie has much in common with other contemporary mystical songwriters.

Photo: Ralph Hulett

**Early performance of Fleetwood Mac with Stevie and Lindsey;
Balboa Stadium 8-31-75**

21

Photo: Jim Welander

Photos: Jim Welander

**Promo photo for Stevie and
Lindsey's only album as a duo
before joining Fleetwood Mac.**

Rare photos of Buckingham Nicks concert. Birmingham, Alabama, August 1974 (following page also).

Photo: Ralph Hulett

Photo: Ralph Hulett

"Blame it on My Wild Heart"

35

36

Photo: Ralph Hulett

Photo: Don Bandel

Photo: Jim Welander

43

'To the Gypsies,
That remain'...

Photo: Nancy Barr-Brandon

Photo: Roger Mullins

Photo: Roger Mullins

49

Photo: Roger Mullins

Photo: Roger Mullins

Photo: Don Bandel

**Fleetwood Mac
Awards
Congratulations**

Photo: Nancy Barr-Brandon

Photo: Don Bandel

Photo: Roger Mullins

Photo: Roger Mullins

Photo: Roger Mullins

Photos: Don Bandel

**A very overweight Stevie during the *Rock-a-little Tour*.
A good example of Stevie's survival instincts to pull
herself out of this condition later.**

Photo: Don Bandel

Photo: Don Bandel

"Let yourself lay back
with in your dream"

Photo: Roger Mullins

Photos: Nancy Barr-Brandon

Photos: Nancy Barr-Brandon

69

Photo: Don Bandel

Photo: Don Bandel

Photo: Roger Mullins

Photo: Don Bandel

Photo: Don Bandel

Photo: Don Bandel

Photo: Don Bandel

Photo: Roger Mullins

Photo: Roger Mullins

Photo: Roger Mullins

Section 2

Lady Of The Stars

I have made the comparison of Stevie Nicks to some of the other writers of today who are doing mystical and related subject material in their songwriting. In my first book I spoke of Van Morrison, Donovan, Kate Bush and others. One person who is exploding on the scene is Tori Amos.

With her two blockbuster albums, *Little Earthquakes* and *Under the Pink.* Tori Amos is proving to be a great, new emerging talent and a match for the likes of the mystical Kate Bush.

Born in North Carolina, the daughter of a Methodist preacher she grew up listening to Fats Waller, Nat King Cole, Jimi Hendrix and John Lennon. *Atlantic Records* says in their bio and press release that she was a gifted child prodigy and could play the piano by the age of two-and-a-half. She was composing musical scores by the age of four. Because of her obvious gift she was the center of attention and in great demand as a performer at social gatherings. She stated that, "It took me some time to come to terms with this. But I grew to realize that I had some kind of calling."

Elvis Presley was known to be obsessed with trying to understand why he was singled out to be so famous with his gift of music. He studied esoteric books searching for the answer.

Tori Amos trained and studied at the Peabody Conservatory in Baltimore before being dismissed for "irreconcilable differences." This was between the ages of five and eleven. The purpose of that school was to train one to be a classical pianist and you had to learn to read music. They did not want her to play by ear, or instinct. Later in her teens she would draw on some of that training by playing Gershwin standards in bars and hotels in Washington, D.C. and Baltimore.

PHOTO CREDIT: CINDY PALMANO

TORI AMOS

Photo: Courtesy Atlantic Records

Singer/Songwriter

It was finally while living in Los Angeles in the mid-80's that Tori began composing her own songs. These would later become the basis for her album *Little Earthquakes.*

Tori Amos explores the spiritual in her songs along with a startling approach of candidness and subject material that is unlike most anything that has been done before. She says in her record company bio that "I don't see myself as weird, I just see myself as honest. That's just the way I am. I find the truth endlessly interesting."

Her candidness in her songs is amazing, reminiscent of John Lennon. In her song *God* from the *Under the Pink* album her lyrics say, "God sometimes you just don't come through ... do you need a woman to look after you?"

✠

Donovan is another mystical songwriter, a real poet of the heart, a real romantic. Although his heyday was in the sixties and early seventies, Donovan continues to write, perform and record. Most of his albums are now produced in Europe. The latest entitled, *One Night in Time.* There is a new maturity tempered with time and experience in his current music. *One Night in Time* has some remarkable moods and musical spells that only Donovan can cast. This writer has had the pleasure of corresponding with Donovan and has done artwork for him. He currently lives in Ireland, a country who has passed special tax laws just to bring in artists, poets and musicians to it's land.

✠

Then there's Kate Bush. In the November 6, 1993 issue of England's *Melody Maker* in an article entitled; *Heaven's Kate* they describe her by saying, "By 1985's *Hounds of Love* (album), Bush had earned a reputation as an art-rock pioneer whose ability to straddle the charts and the avant-garde was second to none."

It is also interesting to see in the same article their comparison to Stevie Nicks, "... (Kate Bush) fueled by visions from

Singer/Songwriter, Dovovan

literature and mythology. Bush's early music and image exude the same kind of wispy pre-Raphealite feminism as Stevie Nicks (another England-obsessed hippy chick); a wild and free femininity, an autonomy achieved not through confrontation but elusiveness."

Kate Bush explores the mystical, the pagan and even shades of Wicca, or Earth religions in her music. One writer who has touched on this area of Kate is Kevin Cann along with Sean Mayes. In their book, *Kate Bush, A Visual Documentary* they expound on this very subject along with great photos of Kate and her history. Published by England's Omnibus Press, it is a book for every fan of Kate's and a very interesting profile.

Kate's latest album, at this writing, is the incredible *Red Shoes*. In it she combines very creative music along with lyrics of Biblical references, vivid imagery and her usual brand of eccentric mysticism. In the same *Melody Maker* article as mentioned before she stated about *Red Shoes,* "Musically, I was just trying to get a sense of delirium, of something very circular and hypnotic, but building and building." The writer goes on to say, "With its mix of acoustic instruments and synth-like keyboard textures, *The Red Shoes* immediately made me think Bush was trying to make a link between ancient and modern ideas of dance, pagan rites and techno-pagan raving."

Kate replied by saying, "Something very similar was on my mind, the idea of trance, delirium, as a way of transcending the normal. Maybe human beings actually need that. Things are very hard for people in this country, maybe they instinctively need to transcend it all. It's very much that ancient call."

In her song *Top of the City* from *The Red Shoes* she has very inspiring lyrics. As she's at 'the top of the city' she says, "I don't know if I'm closer to Heaven but it looks like Hell down there." She makes reference to being put on "angel's shoulders 'on top of the city." I wonder if the song concept could have been inspired by the Bible account of Satan taking

THE SENSUAL WORLD · KATE BUSH

HER NEW SINGLE

Jesus to the top of the city to try to tempt him by saying he would give him all of it if Jesus would worship Satan?

In my first book on Stevie Nicks I made reference to Stevie's song *Gold Dust Woman* and how the writer Jeff Godwin thought that the ending words to the song was a evocation to 'spirits.' In Kate Bush's song, *Lily* there is a evocation at the beginning of the song that is very strange and interesting and, somebody correct me if I'm wrong, but it has to be to some form of Goddess, Wiccan god, or something. The prayer/evocation goes, "Oh thou, who givest sustenance to the universe From whom all things proceed To whom all things return Unveil to us the face of the true spiritual sun (not Son, as in Son of God, as Jesus), Hidden by a disc of golden light That we may know the truth And do our whole duty As we journey to thy sacred feet."

Then the song goes on about the seeker asking for advice from some spiritual counselor. And the interesting thing is the advice this spiritual guru gives, "Child you must protect yourself, I'll show you how with fire." Then the song goes into another prayer/ evocation to angels/ spirits deities for a plea of power and fire. This to me is pure Wicca. It is interesting how Kate is bringing this kind of material to the mainstream through her gift of music.

One other song on her *Red Shoes* album that is exceptional to me is the song, *Why Should I Love You. It* has haunting, beautiful music along with a Pop chorus. A beautiful mystical love song! The credits are quite interesting as well with it listing Kate and **Prince** sharing the arrangement. The song has such a lasting mood created in it that it stays in my mind, the gift that Kate Bush has for writing. The lyrics say, "Have you ever seen a picture of Jesus Laughing? Mmm, do you think He had a beautiful smile? A smile that healed."

Two other songwriters that need to be in this list before

returning to the main subject of Stevie Nicks are the Irish mystic, Van Morrison and newcomer Canadian Loreena McKennitt.

Van Morrison continues to be a prolific songwriter with new albums coming out all the time. he tours constantly and has the reputation of making it "his own way" in the music industry. There are many past stories how Van came up against the music and record company executives head to head on issues and finally won out. He is a uncompromising and eccentric artist. One can even go back to his earliest work with the Irish group he fronted in the sixties, *Them,* to see examples of his spiritual leanings with songs like *Into the Mystic* and *Here Comes The Night.*

Most everyone knows of his mega-hit *Gloria,* but many people are not aware of the many songs, albums and work he has kept producing since then. *Astral Weeks* was one of his most poetic, creative and innovative albums, and voted many times in polls as one of the most original albums of all times. All of his works contain some mystical and spiritual songs, if not the whole album itself devoted to the theme. *Beautiful Vision* is one of the many albums completely filled with songs of a mystical and spiritual nature. Van Morrison continues a personal style of songwriting and subject material that is an inspiration to many other notable music figures like Bob Dylan and Bono of U2.

Finally we come to Loreena McKennitt, probably one of the best kept secrets in the music world as a new emerging artist of incredible talent and vision. Loreena is from Canada and has produced five albums on her own record label. She blends a type of romantic Celtic-Irish music with a contemporary feel. Her 1991 album, *The Visit* was winner of the Juno Award for 'Best Roots and Traditional' album. It achieved double platinum sales in Canada and has been released by *Warner Music Int'l* in over 35 countries worldwide.

**The Irish Mystical
Songwriter: Van Morrison**

Her music on her latest album, *The Mask and Mirror* reminds me of some of Donovan's soundtract music he wrote for the film *Brother Sun, Sister Moon,* the story of St. Francis of Assisi. It also reminds me of the album that Van Morrison recorded of traditional Irish music with the Chieftains. Very incredible music and style! Songs on the album are *The Mystic's Dream, The Bonny Swans.*

Then there is her song *The Dark Night of the Soul* based on lyrics by the 15th century Spanish mystic, St. John of the Cross. Here again she has adapted his writings and arranged it set to her music. The notes from her album concerning the songs are like a spiritual quest diary and a study of history and roots trying to find answers to the things of the soul. In her Introduction she says, "I look back and forth through the window of 15th century Spain, through the hues of Judaism, Islam and Christianity, and was drawn into a fascinating world: history, religion, cross-cultural fertilization."

She then lists some of the people, cultures, religions and teachings that influence her studies, "... the Celtic sacred imagery of trees, the Gnostic Gospels, ... who was God? and what is religion, what spirituality? What was revealed and what was concealed, ... and what was mask and what the mirror?"

Stevie Nicks has much in common with these other songwriters that I have mentioned. There seems to be a new breed of writers searching for spiritual answers that reflect in their songwriting and also reflecting the mood of our culture today. When I was working with Jean Enloe on research I would also listen to the many hours of taped radio interviews that she had on Stevie. I would ask Jean questions about the answers Stevie would give to the many questions asked of her. I asked Jean how she would describe Stevie in a few words and Jean said, "Very strong, spiritual and a survivor." My time working with Jean was very interesting, she had such a collection of things!

Photo: Courtesy Quinlan Road

Singer/Songwriter,
Loreena McKennitt

Just about everything you could imagine on Stevie; rare recordings, bootleg albums of all sorts, candid photographs that I wish I could have used in this book, three actual handwritten poems of Stevie's and one of Stevie's actual hand-done art. Also, a 'Thank you' note from Betty Ford from the time Stevie had stayed at her clinic. Sometimes Jean would also order books for Stevie from another New Age bookstore in Pasadena called Alexandria II while I was there.

Jean and I discussed religion, the teachings; *A Course In Miracles* (which Jean was a firm believer in) and other related things. Jean thought that Stevie's song, *Book of Miracles* was really about the teachings/ book(s); *A Course In Miracles. Jean* seemed to have a obscure conception of God, kind of a god-spirit, very New Age. Jean explained to me about Stevie's concern for world affairs and how Stevie helped in many causes like the American Heart Association, especially after her dad had a heart attack. There are references to work Stevie has done for 'Green Peace' and other ecological causes. And from her new album *Street Angel* Stevie has a song entitled; *Jane,* about the pioneer Jane Goodall and her work studying chimpanzee culture and how it relates to human life. She is a scientist from England and Stevie even performed for a benefit concert for Jane Goodall in Dallas, Texas on October 25, 1991. Jane Goodall's philosophy touches Stevie very deeply in common with Stevie's desire to see mankind treat others, including the animal population to respect as we respect the earth we are in care of. Stevie says in the song to Jane, "Such a little girl ... such a hard life, you could take a challenge ... straight between the eyes, ... in the eyes of the world ... you have done so much."

Of course Stevie helped the City of Hope for their help when her good friend Robin Anderson died of leukemia. In *Arizona Highways* magazine Stevie said, "So to help heart and leukemia research, I give songs away. Well, song royalties, I

Robin Anderson. Stevie's
good friend from High School
who died of Leukemia.

A example
of one of
the benefit
concerts
Stevie
would do
for health
related
charities.

mean. It's my way of contributing to vital research I am incapable of doing myself."

Jean Enloe had said that Stevie is a survivor and I would totally agree. Through health problems, drug dependency, weight problems and areas where she could not cross the line on marriage, children or a career she has survived. Stevie has expressed desires for having her own children so much in the past and could not decide to give up her career for a family, Yet, she says: "I definitely want to have one or two children and I don't want to wait any further than say 34." This quote was from *Teen Magazine* in 1977.

The only marriage Stevie had was the short one to Kim Anderson who was the husband to her good friend Robin. Many people thought it was a bad idea on Stevie's behalf, including Stevie's parents, to marry Kim. Most thought the only reason Stevie did it was to help provide a home for Robin's only son born to Robin and Kim just before Robin's death. The marraige itself was not without intrigue. In Timothy White's *Musician Magazine* article entitled, *Last Tangos New Beginnings* he wrote in February 1989, "Kim Anderson was a member of the Hiding Place Church, whose born-again Christian liturgy emphasized the supernatural and the charismatic. Philip Wagner, the minister who officiated at the January 29, 1983 Anderson-Nicks nuptials, was outspoken in his "trepidation" concerning the pairing, stating he did not know "where Stevie was at with God." Separation papers were filed several months later, the formal divorce coming through in April 1984."

Stevie has expressed regrets many times to the press about her sadness of not having chosen marriage and a family over her career. This seems to be a dilemma that Stevie has been unable to resolve and therefore suffer the emotional crisis it does in her. The publication *Mirror Woman,* January 15, 1992 said, "And yet despite all the trappings of wealth there is an aura of yearning that surrounds Stevie." Later in the same ar-

ticle Stevie is quoted as saying, "I lov
comfortable. My mum is just like that a
from her. But the one thing I haven't ma
her is a lifetime with somebody."

Many people do not know the fact
abortion on a number of occasions. She
in only two sources that I know of. And s... ...as expressed the
deep regret this has caused her, "I love children and children
love me. it is one of my biggest disappointments that I have
not given birth ... The pregnancies had to be terminated because I was in the middle of one of the world's biggest rock
groups ... It was sheer agony for me to make those decisions."

Stevie went on to say how she felt she would be respon-
sible for other people's welfare involved with having the show
on the road stopped with Fleetwood Mac due to her leaving to
have a baby. She went on to say, "But though I might have
stopped wrecking other people's lives in a lot of ways I feel I
ruined my own by not going through with my pregnancies."

The other source that I have where Stevie talks about her
abortions is from *Vox* magazine, February 1992 the British publication. It's interesting that in the beginning "blurb" before
the article the writer says, "... bullied by her record company
..." (I wonder if they were referring to her former management,
the one that I had problems with?) Later in the article it talks
about how she had a dispute about using a song written by Jon
Bon Jovi on her *Timespace* album. The song was *Sometimes
It's a Bitch* and Stevie objected to using it for a number of
reasons. Stevie says in the article, "I know that just me singing
that kind of song wasn't going to go over with a lot of my fans,
which it hasn't. But I was told by the industry, by **management**
(my emphasis), by the record companies, and by everybody
else, that if I did NOT do this, and reach this new audience that
my career was simply, finally, completely over."

In the *Vox* article the writer talks about how Timespace's

es were full of references to her ex-lovers. The article n to say, "Was there a common thread among her men? ey are all very smart and very loving, and they all had a difficult time with my life ... For four lovers, a crucial test came when she became pregnant and opted for terminations. "It's always been a tragedy. But they understood But they didn't really."

The *Vox* writer said that Stevie finally had to decide to put her career and her fans before a relationship of permanence with any of the men. he went on to write, "But now there is remorse at the havoc her abortions have wreaked on her psyche. "to give up four (babies) is to give up a lot that would be here now. So that really bothers me, a lot, and really breaks my heart. But, they're gone, so ..."

In that article by Timothy White, *Last Tangos, New Beginnings,* that I referred to earlier Stevie is quoted as saying, "They say that from tragedy comes great art ... Sometimes I think I should go back to being a waitress; maybe I would enjoy life more. But if I led a perfectly-existing life, where I didn't try the universe or dare anybody or take any risks, I would never have written all those songs! So in all of us there's some great tragedy that has gone on, and that is what we write about."

It seems like Stevie has made a move to take back some control over her career by leaving her former management and going with long time friends and co-workers Glen Parrish. Her new album *Street Angel* seems to be an indication of this smart move. I consider the album a sparkling production. It's a very tight album to me with no loose, dead spaces. The songwriting is solid. her one cut, *Listen to the Rain* has to me the same dynamic punch as the Rolling Stones 70's album *It's Only Rock & Roll.* Each song is well done to me and I consider it one of her best solo albums to date.

On *Greta* it says that, "She's got her bags packed ... And

Street Angel
Tour Photos

Street Angel
Tour Photos

Photos: Don Bandel

101

Photo: Don Bandel

Street Angel
Tour Photos

Photos: Don Bandel

Photo: Don Bandel

**Stevie entering WNEW-FM
Radio station, NYC to
promote *Street Angel*.**

105

**Stevie entering back stagedoor
of the David Letterman show
to promote *Street Angel*.**

Photo: Don Bandel

she's off to the valley where the sun meets the sea, You understand that she wants to live by the ocean ... And no one is pleased She gets a house in the mountains ..." Considering that Stevie has mentioned in interviews how her songs are many times based on her own experiences it could be that this song is very autobiographical, even though it's supposed to be about the late film star Greta Garbo. In my first book I referred to a quote about how Stevie went to the beach to live to find solace after her good friend, Robin Anderson died. Her reference to a "house in the mountains" could be her house on Camelback Mountain in Scottsdale, Arizona. Or, am I making the mistake of weaving meanings into lyrics that I am not sure of the meanings? This was done, of course, on the great *Paul (McCartney) Is Dead* fiasco during the Beatles heyday. But again, this is what is so interesting about art and poetry — is that there are many meanings to different people in a work.

Her song *Destiny* as I mentioned in the introduction is an exceptionally good song to me and seems to capture Stevie's world-view very well. The whole album is outstanding.

To sum up this writing on Stevie Nicks I like what she said in a recent interview with The *Boston Globe* writer, Steve Morse, "It's hot here (Phoenix, Arizona, at her home), it's 106 degrees today. But when the sun goes down, I sit outside and it's so beautiful. If you have any problems, you go outside and they disintegrate. I've grown to really depend on my desert-sky time ... I guess that's why the Indians became very spiritual, because it's very easy to get into a spiritualistic kind of mode here."

In another related quote Stevie had this to say about her Arizona home in Arizona Highways Magazine, "I was born on this desert, and I'm still a desert baby. Desert is very healing to me, and my Phoenix home is where I go to write songs and let the creative juices flow ... There is something about the piano, the view of Camelback Mountain, my home — well, I get there and suddenly songs begin to happen. You don't stop them when they occur to you or they are gone forever."

As I stated in my introduction I have written this book a little different than my first one. I have presented many sides and aspects of Stevie from my experience and research, both positive and negative, trying to be objective.

I still see Stevie Nicks as a great talent, a gifted poet, survivor and songwriter. When I was working with Jean Enloe Jean had offered me her own manuscript of a book that she was working on as well. She offered to let me take it back to Tulsa if I had wanted to use any of her research and writings. Sadly, Jean passed away from her heart condition before seeing the completion of the first book. This book, as the first one was, is dedicated to her.

THE END

Photo: Don Bandel

More *Street Angel*
Tour Photos

Photo: Don Bandel

Photo: StarFile

Photo: StarFile

Acknowledgements

Again, as with my first book on Stevie Nicks, there were many people involved who helped me complete this project.

Thanks to Jack Wynn, of WYNNPUBLISHING, for wanting to do the book, for reprinting the first book (and for having patience when I went over schedule on time). "I'm hurrying as fast as I can Jack."

Thanks to Larry Shaeffer of Little Wing Productions for giving me my start in book publishing. Thanks to Charlie Jennemann and Tony Secunda on the first book even though we weren't able to complete it together.

Thanks to all the fans and people who helped me with research materials, Virginia Lohle of StarFile, Jan Adams, Bud Hart, Joe Sia, Sue Cole, Don Bandel, Marc Mathers, Sheri Booth for being a big S.N. fan and for your support, Kristi for the hospitality, Lisa Carrier, Johanna Pieterman and Jim Welander.

Thanks to Nancy Barr-Brandon, Ralph Hulett, James A. Christjohn, and to all the other people who I may have forgotten. And special thanks to the readers for getting the book and for all the nice letters and commments on the first book.

Resource Materials

Since I know fans are great collectors and like to find items of their favorite stars, I've compiled a list of the Fan Clubs, Fan publications, dealers, illustrators and photographers which I recommend.

Fan Clubs and Publications:

* *Frozen Love*
  Johlande Groenenboom
  Elritsstraat 75
  3192 CB Hoogvliet RT
  The Netherlands

* *Affairs of the Heart*
  Molendreef 10
  461 CW Ossendrecht
  The Netherlands

* *Dreaming Fairies*
  (Stevie/ Kate Bush zine)
  Peter Borbe
  Mindener Str. 43
  W-2841 Wagenfeld
  Germany

* *Fleetwood Mac/
  Stevie Fanzine*
  A. Foley
  46 St. John's Ave.
  Clondalkin
  Dublin 22
  Ireland

* *To write Stevie:*
  STEVIE NICKS
  P.O. Box 6907
  Alhambra, CA 91802
  USA

* For authentic Stevie
  items and autographed mer-
  chandise:

  Silver Spring Emporium
  102 S. Beeline Hwy.
  Payson, AZ 85541
  USA

* Fan Mail, Official
  Fan Club (As listed on
  Street Angel):
  7605 Santa Monica Blvd.
  #721
  West Hollywood, CA 90046
  USA

Illustration & Photo Credits

Photographers:

Joe Sia: Page 10.
955 Tunxis Hill Rd., Fairfield, CT 06430, USA.

Jim Welander: Pages 17, 20, 22, 23, 24, 25, 32, 37, 41
114 East Linclon, Fergus Falls, MN 56537, USA.

Ralph Hulett: Pages 19, 30, 33 (bottom), 35, 36 (top), 39, 42, 45.
P.O. Box 2304, Costa Mesa, CA 92628, USA.

Kat: Pages 27, 28.
Kathy Twadell, 409 S. Main #1, Independence, MO 64050, USA

StarFile: Pages 31, 33 (top), 105, 114, 115.
11 West 20th St., 7th floor, New York, NY 10011, USA

Nancy Barr-Brandon: Pages 36 (bottom), 43, 46, 54, 55, 68, 69.
506 Windermere Ave., Interlaken, NJ 07712, USA

Don Bandel: Pages 40 (top), 53, 56, 62, 63, 64, 65, 70, 71, 74, 75, 76, 77, 99, 100, 101, 102, 103, 104, 106, 107, 112, 113.
40 Willow St. #B, Bayonne, NJ 07002, USA

Roger Mullins: Pages 48, 49, 50, 51, 58, 59, 60, 67, 72, 78, 79, 80.
c/o Wynn Pub, P.O. Box 1491, Pickens, SC 29671, USA

Bud Hart: Page 89.
7220 Riverview Ave., Edgely, PA 19007, USA

Illustrators:

Johanna Pieterman: Pages Intro, 21, 47, 57, 61, 73, 92, 116.
c/o Pr. Julianstraat 22, 4424 AV Wemeldinge, The Netherlands

Lisa Carrier: Pages 29, 34, 38, 44, 52, 66, 108, 122.
P.O. Box 434, Hollywood, CA 90078, USA

Marc Mathers: Page 40.

Ed Wincentsen: Page 84.

Also Available From Wynn Publishing!

LYNYRD SKYNYRD
"GIMME BACK MY BULLETS"
Original Concert UK Tour Book
(#11938) - $25.00

FLEETWOOD MAC
International Tribute/Commemorative Program
from '92 Austin Convention - ONLY 300 MADE!
(#20423) - $25.00

LED ZEPPELIN
AN EVENING WITH...
1977 Original Concert Tour Book
(#11937) - $20.00

JIM MORRISON
"IMAGES OF JIM MORRISON"
Book by Ed. Wincentsen
(#32421) - $10.00

STEVIE NICKS
"ROCK'S MYSTICAL LADY"
Revised Edition - Now 122 pages!
by Ed. Wincentsen
(#32422) - $15.00

STEVIE NICKS
"LADY OF THE STARS"
Book by Ed. Wincentsen
(#32423) - $15.00

EAGLES
1976 Original Concert Tour Book
(#11902) - $15.00

STEVIE NICKS
"WILD HEART"
Original Concert Tour Book
(#11953) - $75.00

STEVIE NICKS
High School Yearbook Reprint
ONLY 300 NUMBERED
COPIES
(#25643) - $35.00

STEVIE NICKS
'TIMESPACE'
Original Concert Tour Book
(#20041) - $30.00

STEVIE NICKS
"ROCK A LITTLE"
Original Concert Tour Book
(#11952) - $25.00

HEART
"PASSIONWORKS"
Original Concert Tour Book
(#11929) - $25.00

HEART
"BAD ANIMALS"
Original Concert Tour Book
(#11926) - $15.00

HEART
"BRIGADE"
Original Concert Tour Book
(#11928) - $15.00

OLIVIA NEWTON-JOHN
"PHYSICAL"
Original Concert Tour Book
(#11954) - $40.00

MADONNA
"BLONDE AMBITION"
Original Concert Tour Book
(#11940) - $20.00

MADONNA
"WHO'S THAT GIRL"
Original Concert Tour Book
(#11941) - $20.00

STEVIE NICKS
EUROPEAN IMPORT CALENDAR
11 3/4 x 16 1/2 Full Color
British Calendar
(#32424) - $15.00

STEVIE NICKS
"ROCK A LITTLE"
11x17 Original Concert Tour
Poster from Austin, TX
(#31619) - $12.00

STEVIE NICKS
"OTHER SIDE OF
THE MIRROR"
11x17 Original
Concert Tour Poster
from Austin, TX
(#31621) - $12.00

STEVIE NICKS
"WILD HEART"
11x17 Original Concert Tour
Poster from Austin, TX
(#31622) - $14.00

FLEETWOOD MAC
"RUMOURS"
Original Concert Tour Book
(#11914) - $50.00

Wynn Publishing books are available in many of the finer bookstores. If you have any difficulty
getting the book(s) you want, write to us at:

WYNN PUBLISHING
PO BOX 1491SB
PICKENS, SC
29671

List the items numbers and quantities you want. Please add $4 for Priority shipping or $6 for Insured Priority shipping
on any size order. South Carolina residents please add 5% sales tax. We accept Visa, MasterCard, Discover and
American Express. To place a phone order, please call us at 803/878-6469. To place a fax order, dial 803/878-6267.

"I see my reflection in your eyes"